© Dorian Culver
All Rights Reserved
Reproduction of the whole
or any parts of the contents
without permission
is prohibited.

Printed in the United States of America
ISBN 978-0-6925886-9-7
First Edition: 2015

THE BEAUTY WE GET LOST IN

The Beauty We Get Lost In

Dorian Culver

The Beauty We Get Lost In, is a collection of poetry written over the span of multiple years. This writing highlights feelings, sentiments, and observations regarding various seasons and stages of life.

Whether we recognize the beauty that is around us or feel as though we are estranged from it, there is still deeper we must go in our experience.

This collection is dedicated to everyone who is on a journey to find deeper meaning as they embrace the beauty hidden in life.

-The prayer below was written by an anonymous author.

It not only captures the thoughts of the fishermen who've prayed it, but it also captures the essence of how many people approach life in general.

The world itself is so big, and we as people, are small.

Breton Fishermen's Prayer

"Dear God, be good to me; The sea is so wide, And my boat is so small."

-Anonymous-

The Beauty We Get Lost In

Part I:
The Sea Also Rises: We are often lost and in need of rescue.

Part II:

In Our Masks We Trust: We are often not our most true selves

Part III:

Beauty Awakened: There is beauty all around us

Part IV:

Lost in Love: In love we are lost, rescued, and fulfilled.

Though we are surrounded by an abundance of beauty,
we often find ourselves lost in it.

The beauty we get lost in drowns us in the shallow end

I: The Sea Also Rises

Unseen

I can't unsee
the things
I've seen,
They scream too
LOUD
within my
soul now

Scars

I'm bearing the scars from marks that I've missed,
reminiscing my timeline, recalling my trysts

Emaciated

Emaciated, starving, and hungry
are the kids in some of our streets
Parents pawned their last possessions for bags to keep up the habit

This is the hood they live in,

Where taxpayers are mad 'cause they're picking up slack from bad decisions

And

Kids aren't able to eat, wishing parents would change the ways of their shame,
and into the light they could retreat,

But,

This is the hood they live in

Bankrupt educational systems

Poverty stricken

Living below prime economic conditions

We see what they've been given

We see

 Kids resorting to drugs, succumbing to the pleas of the hood's thugs.

 Misused and confused, they abuse the substance to fill in the lack of love

We see the need to make a difference

because these neighborhoods cover the earth.

And that should make us different

For,

These are the hoods WE live in

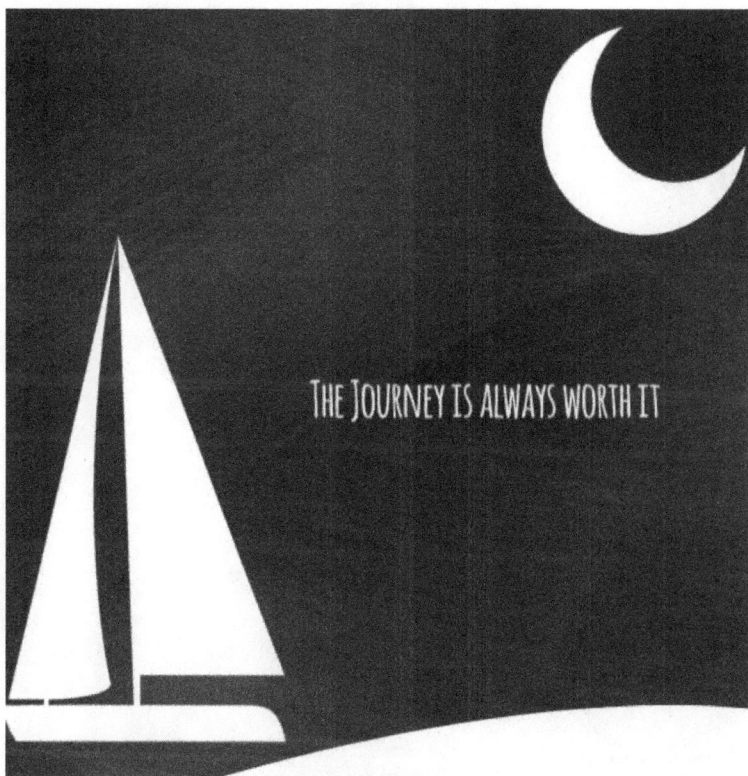

THE JOURNEY IS ALWAYS WORTH IT

She

She
is more than what she seems
beneath the seams
she is broken

She
is drowning in an ocean of emotion
but she's coping

We Scream

We scream a chorus, and everyone ignores us…

****
****

-To be ignored, denied, or overlooked is one of the most frustrating realities that exists.

We as people crave being heard, accepted, and validated.

I want to assure you that you not only have a voice, but you have an audience that is watching and listening.

Not everyone will value what you have, but the right people will, and that alone is worth it.

So use your talents, your time, and your creativity to tell your story.

You will find that so much that is lost in the word around you, will be recovered by you being authentically you.

Runaway

Runaway

     Where are you running today?—

Only God knows where at last you'll stay.

Runaway

 Why are you running today?—

Is life too complicated for you to say?

Runaway

When will you come back our way?—

Home is only footsteps away.

-We are running.

So often we run and put ourselves under the command of whatever we think can save us or make us happy.

Often the beautiful things in this life are hidden in things that don't seem outwardly appealing. Things like faith, hard work, and sacrifice.

This has been the case for generations.

Living different takes courage.

My Daughter

You refused to be ashamed—

The rotted carrion of your casualties line trophy rooms in Hell. You're under a spell of arrogance and your drunkenness bleeds into the heart of the people.

Upon every high mountain and under every green tree—you've lain with strange men—your harlotry bleeds. A fearless, earless, careless daughter—Won't you return from playing a harlot?

Wounded and scarred—the people are poisoned with passivity's garb.

The broken pieces of moral minded resolve are scattered in the lowest places abroad—invisible bars—have captured understanding.

A fearless, earless, zeal-less, daughter—Won't you return from playing a harlot?

Return: "…'Yet, even now,' declares The Lord,

'Return to me with all your heart…'

…for He is gracious and merciful,

slow to anger and abounding in steadfast love;

and He relents over disaster."

Joel 2:12-13

Institutionalism

Institutionalism keeps us bound with invisible bars—

killing our vitality with invisible scars from wounds long past—

that are poured through stolen stories

pierced by unimaginable maladies

passing through cable cars

we travel through tragedy

We wonder why the caged bird no longer sings

and the bedrest is paradise for weary souls.

We wonder why we crave sleep like a drug, and stagger toward an immersion of reality —

We long for better days

Fairytales dripping with escape.

We wonder why we allow ourselves to live our lives

Institutionalized,

When we could be free

Patchwork Heart

We have these little patchwork hearts.

They have been marginalized and manipulated.

Marred and mangled.

Painfully put to shame,

At times, they've been shredded to pieces beyond recognition,

But the fabric of those fragments have come together

And forged a material

stronger than ever.

Out To Sea

If we'll just set out to sea
Well see more than
what we seek

Icy Blue Tear: Icy blue tear

Why won't you come down?

Pound by bloated pound

Hidden in a mystery

Your symphony resounds—

Kept back by mother's fears

Made captive through the years—

When alas might you depart from me, you awkward from of manhood?

Unknown the way you should be,

Even with the weakness within me

I long for you to come…So come to me

And let your silent slickness streak along my nerve endings as you slowly roll right down my cheek.

I am nervous now to even imagine what could be.

You're taking a hold of me.

Exposed and known, I offer myself to you…

Here I am, icy blue tear,

You fall…

again and again you fall

…again, and again, and again,

 I'm free

At War

Before we ever went out on playgrounds to swing

    Or built sandcastles in the sand

Or learned our ABC's and how to count to ten,

    we were little boys and little girls at war

We were at war with systems that attempted to silence our unique voices and have us conform to the status quo

We were at war to not lose ourselves in pain and heartbreak or even the trivial matters of the day

We were at war to avoid being gripped by vices that sought to expose our weaknesses and savagely destroy us

We were little boys and little girls at war

Who had to fight for our future to become who we truly are

And

To find a way to use our gifts in a market place that says "We already have someone who does what you do."

We've been at war to rise up and take action, and stand against injustice, when so many other little boys and girls grew up to be men and women who did not.

We've been at war to become an authentic voice in a world saturated with impostors

We've been at war seeking out souls who are lost, confused and hurting, to heal them

We've been at war to find those who hurt them

And do our best to make sure they never hurt anyone else again

And sometimes we are at war within ourselves

Every time we look in the mirror and we don't like what we see, we are at war

Every time we question our existence and we just can't find a "Why" or a "What", we are at war

Every time we examine ourselves and we think, "I just don't measure up." We are at war

Every time we search for answers, and find none.

Those are all wars

As often as we've done anything else

we've been fighting wars to achieve greatness,

and to better ourselves and our loved ones,

and impact the world around us.

Though no armor has been foisted upon us,

we are fighting battles everyday

right where we are

"Be kind; everyone you meet is fighting a hard battle."

-Ian Maclaren-

We Are Broken

Broken

I'm such a broken man
with broken dreams,
broken stories and
broken plans.

Pages

Who else can I be honest with if not these pages, for I am living in-
between the lines of broken chapters,
looking for laughter

Icarus

We get so high in the sky sometimes,
We soar to the realm of the sun.
Then like us, our Icarus wax wings. They run.

Pretty Face Cold Heart: Pretty face, cold heart

What was thought of as love--

quickly fell apart.

Seeking with deceptive intentions,

heartache from silly traditions,

you never get back what you put in,

so turn away from this invention.

I sought after her,

her thoughts enveloped my mind,

I thought she was the one for me

Until I finally found

The fallacy of fulfilled hope

Is possessing what's pursued,

'cause now I have her, but I don't want her

Now I *know* her, but I don't *like* her,

And I regret the day I ever *met* her.

This is the destructiveness of attractiveness,

 if we judge content by its appearance.

The anomaly of frivolity, mistaking the lure of lust for quality

Turn away from man's methods or face the same calamity.

Poison Heart

(An Excerpt)

And her loving heart was
swallowed by an
empty space
where bitterness ate
through her flesh

Blind Spring

Though
friendly with the season's pages when they turned,
she was far too cordial with slumber
to notice what blossomed.

-We don't trust what we cannot see, but often what we can't see, is a beautiful mystery soon to be revealed. Don't fear the blackness.

Black

Bleak black night
the tide retracts for you
the stars burn with fury
and live beside the moon

Fragile Lives

When will we realize
There's fragile lives
Behind these fragile eyes

Our words are powerful.

They carry weight.

I can still remember the powerful things that people have spoken to me from years and years ago.

Though there have been so many good and encouraging things spoken, it seems that negative things can be recalled so easily.

There are certain things that stick out and are hard to forget.

Is it the same for you?

The fact is, we all have a sphere of influence in the lives of the people around us, and our actions and even our words can literally affect their destiny. Please remember, not everyone can be you or do what you do.

Show grace.

Try to see the good in everyone.

Use your voice and platform to promote, encourage, motivate and heal.

There are tons of people that just need to be loved and treated delicately. There are fragile lives behind these fragile eyes.

Part II: In Our Masks We Trust

Masks

In our masks we trust
like phantoms of lust
We seek and we find
alternate lives.
Between
fantasy
and
reality
we walk the line
We have our fill of wildness
as we steal the night
Hungover mornings
until we see the sun rise
We lose sight of ourselves
we give darkness a life
Professing to have answers
we teach treacherous lies
put off by sobriety
until the day that we die
We've sullied our faces
time after time
We've ensnared ourselves
with duplicitous ties
Trusting the figments
we make in our minds
 We're afraid to be naked,
but the naked are wise.

This Life

I'd be lying
if I said this life wasn't trying
First I'm fighting,
then flying
Then feel like I'm dying
I'm diving
into the limitless river
that washes up
understanding
I've been trying to face my face in the mirror
But it's demanding
To be candid
I'm a man
But it's
Really hard to handle,
I see these celebrities on TV,
they keep flying off the handle
then they're falling into scandals
But their life
won't light a candle to my vices
I'm an animal
Why do you think they call me Hannibal?
Because I'm nice when in the light
But, Who am I at night
with all the Hellish things I like?
I cannot write my wrongs
even though
I am contrite
I'm still a thief
loving the night
And so it's for these wrongs
I write

Portraits:

The Well

Maybe we are all just women at the well,
having a flood of undiscovered lovers,
romancing a shell of our true selves.

Davids

Maybe we are all King David's
hiding on rooftops
instead of fighting our battles
lusting for
damsels
in convenient
places

Adams and Eves

Maybe we are Adams and Eves

Trusting the lust of forbidden fruit

Damned with knowledge

Running reckless

Naked

Hiding from a loving God

Apostle Pauls

Maybe we are Apostle Pauls

broken by the scandals of our past,

trading power and prestige

to humbly preach the Gospel

to every ear who would hear

a sinner saved by Grace

Fetching Attention

Her heart never felt rest
It was dormant at best
She coquettishly fetched attention,
she was as desperate as the rest

Brother Man

We run ourselves into the ground
We've run aground
with empty promises
Ambitious
As
those
who seek
the crown

We bend corners but we don't slow down…

We're run down

Tired and thirsty,
full of angst and ire

Until we burn out.

We say,

"Oh, We'll sleep when we die…" But it's a lie,
And we don't mind entertaining them.

Somehow we know there's trouble because
we're passive when we should be acting,
active when we should be passive,
waiting for manna we perform enchanted dances.

We serve ourselves as if we can't see
that we don't even know our brother man.

We look across the aisle, but when eyes on faces not like ours meet,

they soon depart.

We smile and chalk it up to being not the least bit acquainted,
shots are fired,
In our brothers direction,
again, and again.

And we thought we were making progress;
we were just starting to mend.

And at times were bitter,
broken
and jaded,
So we bail out when things get tough.

When things get real
we escape and we feel justified,

But time is flying by.

We cannot change the hands of cards we're dealt
and we can't remain idle
As if we have no hands to help.

This is the web we weave,
the picture that we've painted
we've integrated a face that faces the problems of people
But then unfaithfully we forsake them.

We instead affix labels on people that they were never meant to
carry.

It's scary…

We say "they're the ones that laugh, and sneer, and judge."
We say "they're too sinful, too broken, …"
"We say they are the worthless…"

So we pull back the hedges,
or look across the aisle,
or over the fence,
or across the tracks,
but we dare not get close enough to actually touch.

To actually make a difference.

We ignore our brother man's problems with no explanation
Our hesitation to love
is its own decapitation.

-When we are scarred, it proves that our wounds have healed-

Word Scars

These word scars

Carry lives on the tips of knives

They cut sharp like cheddar

Run red like wine

MIA:

Missing in Action

We keep missing the chance to hold each other dear,

Loving is hard,

When together,

We are everywhere else

But

here

Haiku:

(17 syllables)

She Ran

She ran from her fears
Fought back rivers of tears as
Hope ran from her heart

Common Words

Our common words were wasted in transition

   when they could have passionately started a fire

Apologies

"It can't be fixed!"

She cried as she ran out of the room.

It was worse than she originally thought

He was totally consumed

Though,

He had a penchant for finding just the right words to say.
And he was the king of speaking flirtatious banter,
but on this day,
it did not matter.

Today He could have been the King of England or a homeless man
on the street.

No, it couldn't be fixed.

Today she was tired of carrying the pain of arguments past.

She was tired of nurturing lonely nights--
It had become too hard to lay her head on an empty bed.

She couldn't any longer bear to meticulously explain away details she knew didn't make sense.

So weary of attempting to squeeze truth from loveless lies.
Turing blind eyes to tell-tale signs

It was a hurt that showed in the heaviness in her eyes and the slouch in her shoulders.

It was a hurt that flared up in the condition of her skin.

It unraveled the fibers of her clothing.
As she herself, was unraveling day by day.

And the ear-deafening blasts of a home filled with absence, grew louder and louder.

Today it couldn't be fixed,
for the cool calculated head that normally sat upon her shoulders had now grown hot with scorn.

And her loving heart was swallowed by an empty space where bitterness ate through her flesh

She had been dying a slow death
living with pain that gnawed on her organs like a virus.
And she wondered if she would find happiness again.

She pondered the course of divorce
countless times in the recesses of her mind,
but when she spoke it lead to
a discourse of words that
turned to intercourse
And she soon
changed
course
And those thoughts never saw the light of
day.
But today, it was different

● ● ●

She was not put off of by the stench
of gasoline covering the hints of perfume on his neck and collar.
They were mingled together so carelessly, like they were perishable
and non-perishable goods scattered in the same aisle at the grocery
store

 She felt like the tempest was endless

She could not forgive him…

So today would be different

The kind of vexation
that makes hair grow thin,
finger nails brittle and break,
and sleep escape
was drawing this conclusion for her…

It can't be fixed

Stones Throw

We're just a stones throw away from shattering the glass houses we're caged in.

Lust is a Fire

Lust is a fire
that burns by day
and ravages by night

Designed with desire,
it's never fully consumed
and it doesn't grow tired

It's insidious history
hidden in the mystery of Eden
stores up things that moths
and locusts have habitually eaten

Lust is a fire

Prized as a crowned jewel
heavily adorned in black-tie attire
acquiring things that are briefly admired,
It steals the hearts of all of its buyers
It heaps crowns on the head
of its Hell-ridden supplier

Lust is a fire

Hard-wired
to build empires
that turn good men into liars
Heavily taxing on those whom
it hires
it conspires to attack
when strong men have grown tired…

and nothing less should be expected whenever it's pursued,

for,

Lust is a fire
Lust is a fire
Lust is a FIRE!…looking for *fuel*

Live Free

I'm going to take what you said out

of my ears right now

and let it burn

See,

You don't have the ability to define me

I'm going to unthink your thoughts

And unlabel these boxes

that you've put me in

You saw me simple, like a meme,

fooled yourself into thinking

stereotypes are supreme

But

You can't define me any longer,

So just know

that I live

free

So Many Questions

I have so many questions inside me,

Like where do I go from here?

Is it faith or fear?

Am I the stage or the actor?

Masquerade or the masquer?

Many times I've been the benefactor

Of spectacular disasters

As a matter of fact

Some days I look back and I ask

"Is there any good in what I've done?"

I don't know the evil answers or the outcome

And so I run

Trying to duck and dodge

Every silver bullet from a gun

Bang Bang!

And now I hang onto questions unanswered

I'm still here

Without fear

happily

ever-asking.

Come Apart

We've become accustomed to living in the dark,
so we come apart when we face the
compartments of the heart

Part III: Beauty Awakened

Awakened

When awakened
 by the Artist,
it's an art to depart from the darkness
I embark on a dream like Martin
Like Paul, with a mission I am marked in the eyes of the world like
a starving artist
My heart was hardest in the garden because I did not know who
God was
I was seeking applauses
I was self medicating causes
I was flexing but I wasn't flawless
I was the first Adam, from God my heart I guarded
I did not want to get at Him
I wanted to put my sin on a billboard and worship it -
I was one of the Mad Men
But when I finally got it
He put life in my mortal carcass
Now I see light shining in that darkness
and I am engaged when I'm on theses stages
I'm setting these places ablaze with the aim to make Him famous
I'm not in it for entertainment
I don't get lost in the sea of faces
I've never claimed it's a crime
to be named among the nameless
But I keep sharpening my axe
So I know that steel
stays stainless

Summer

I can barely behold the beauty of sunlit summers.

The radiance of day captured by hunters.

I've seen skies filled with birds taking flight.

Fireflies illuminating star-clothed nights, and I wonder...

Will this beauty endure or someday be cast asunder?

The Window

The window mirrors my life--
hopes to be and dreams to come,
peering through the pane of opportunity,
standing tall in the corridors of possibility--
on the pulse of awakening --perceiving purpose.

The window mirrors my life--
Sitting, watching and waiting--in hopes
that opportunity will befall me--
the call that never comes, the response never written,
the visitation never requested--I'm at the dock of disappointment,
but on the brink of change.

The window mirrors my life--
but I'm not allowing the apprehension of disadvantage to
stagnate progression—or accepting the success
of failure when it frustrates my aspirations.

The window mirrors my life,
because it reflects me--until I realized
I'm now on the other side of the window,
looking at who I used to be.

Dreams

Dreams are
Clear vision in the presence of darkness
Artwork in the hands of gifted artisans
Perception in the minds of the confused
Love in the hearts of the abused
Respect in the attitudes of the neglected
Concern in the bosom of the hated
Purpose in the hands of the talentless
Forgiveness on the shoulders of the outcast
Humility in the pocket of the rich
Health in the lap of the sick
Ability in the life of the disabled
Value in the sight of the worthless
Might on the breast of the weak
Meekness in the might of the strong And
Desire for them all.

He has given us dreams
and they are
the true measurement of faith--
so keep dreaming.

On the Perimeter of Quiet

On the perimeter of quiet
thoughts are loud with persistence
memories are lullabies and dreams dragonflies
on the perimeter of quiet

On the perimeter of quiet
chirps of morning birds are heard
and the emblazoning passion of a
smiling sun is felt
on the perimeter of quiet

On the perimeter of quiet
thoughts are captured and made to
dance in the synchronization of
pulsating rhythm.

On the perimeter of quiet
I can perceive
me

Still Life

Being still,

I can hear—being quiet,

I understand...the clamor

that washes away calm,

the calamity which strives

to enter peace—the coolness

of collection that provides

order and stability. The stillness brings

food for thought—beauty

for ashes—solitude bred

by ration and patience by

instruction.

Still life,

is still,

life.

The Life Inside the Sea

The life inside the sea

Is as diverse as a mystery

rehearsed as a symphony

Monochromatic splashes attract an infinity of symmetry.

The blue-warm ebbs and flow war at the surface—

Iridescent rainbows make bright the crests of waves—they rage
with aggression.

Untamed and raw—they swallow up creation —there is no
comprehending the seas eternity—its conception is in it's coming
up to breath—It's timeless production spoken aloud throughout
history. An ageless masterpiece interwoven into tapestry—a
driving force whipping against land like an enemy—we dive into
this limitless sanctuary

To live life forever, for we are alive inside the sea.

When I am Real

Myself, when I am real

Feels real still.

It is known like a mother to a newborn.

It is quaint and frank

And sometimes silent

Like a night.

Myself, when I am real

Feels beautiful

Like the rays of sunshine

That glimmer through a window at

The opening of day.

 Myself when I am real

Is often cool, calm and collected.

Not striving. Not even daring.

Just being.

It is often tough to get to and

Tough to face

Myself when I am real.

But I am only truly myself

When

 I am

-We see the sun faithfully hang in the sky everyday.

We enjoy it's warmth.

We let it light our way.

The sun keeps us alive day in and day out.

 It retires on schedule every night and plays the background to the moon and stars.

And then it awakens from it's scheduled slumber and relentlessly begins a new day.

It does not fret, or complain.

The sun is loyal to the sky.

It rises to show it's face again and again.-

-Just because we are accustomed to seeing something often, does not make it less intriguing, or less complex, or less amazing.

It makes it more so, because the beauty is that it keeps happening.

The days we get are gifts. Gifts that we are free to unwrap and enjoy everyday.

But they are measured gifts.

How will you use yours today?-

Sunrise

There is a place, and it is not too far off

where dreams reside.

It is a place enchanted with mystery.

A place upholstered with history,
filled with the radiance of rainbows and tickled with the joy of the
heavens.

Where fear and hope collide

It is a place where prayer and faith arise and spawn generations of
destiny.

It is a place burgeoning with new opportunities.

It is a place where pride dies, and a whole new world comes to life.

It is the opposite of sunset.

It is sunrise.

Sugar

Sifting the sugar back into imagination

The sweet stuff that life is made of is

Screaming to be seen

Reality is rarely noticed

when fantasy is bursting at the seams

The balance of life hangs between jet black

nightmares and

soft white dreams

lovingly lulled to sleep

we thrive when were engaged

and rarely miss a beat,

maybe we're misguided,

Alices lost in wonderlands

But when we create with our souls and our hearts and our minds,

We will become younger

We will become alive

We'll know our purpose

And why

Where Goes the Sun

Where goes the sun?

It runs,

hidden by the radiance of night

Clothed with vesper; the day breaks, clouds part and a thousand birds take flight.

Where goes the sun?

It fights.

It burns strong to stay alive,

hangs itself high

It survives the hands of clocks,

until the stars intrude its watch.

But where is the Son of Man?

He shines brighter than the brightest star

He's seen from afar,

He was sought throughout the ages, prognosticated by the sages…

Unlike the sun, He is ageless

Where is the Son of Man?

He sits higher than the highest heights,

His reach transcends the longest days,

His love reflects the light.

Where is the Son of Man?

For wherever He is---There is life!

Masterpieces

They will know our masterpieces
For they are
imagination's pieces brilliantly performing
genius

****

-We ourselves are masterpieces.

Carefully crafted. Designed with a purpose.

We are the canvas the artist is dying to use.

We are beautiful,

and beauty itself is reeling us in.-

Words Wrapped Around Flesh

At best,

We are

Words wrapped around flesh.

Composed of

beautiful phrases that emanate

from our skin and bones

Our deep truths

quake from the pits of our hearts

and the cores of our souls.

Our choruses play slow

during our exits and entrances

Yes,

At best,

We are words

Wrapped around flesh,

And we speak them into existence

Until The day

our ashes return

to the Earth

And our words take on

A life of their own

-If we settle at the safety of the shore and do nothing else, we have lost ourselves. Love compels us to take a journey, and pour out love on those we meet along the way.-

-Stories…

keep telling your stories; they have authority.

No one can dispute what you've seen, or experienced, or felt. No one at all.

You were qualified at birth to tell them and nothing you do will ever disqualify you

from sharing them.

Your thoughts, your feelings, and your perspective have power.

You have been given such a unique storyline. Your stories are fresh. Your stories have value.

And you must keep telling them, because people are drawn to stories with faces.

And they make you

authentically…

you-.

Stories with Faces

We've now become a story
Each one of us
Young and old
Humorous or wise
We are stories with faces
That draw
Attention
And occupy
nuances with identity

True Stories

These words were
able to emerge with grace from fables and fairy tales.
And become
true stories

Maestro

We are notes in a moving symphony
And God is the maestro

We See Beauty

We are the kind that see beauty in the simplest symmetry
We detail an infinity of intricacies that confound the mind
They resound like a symphony
They are sight to the blind

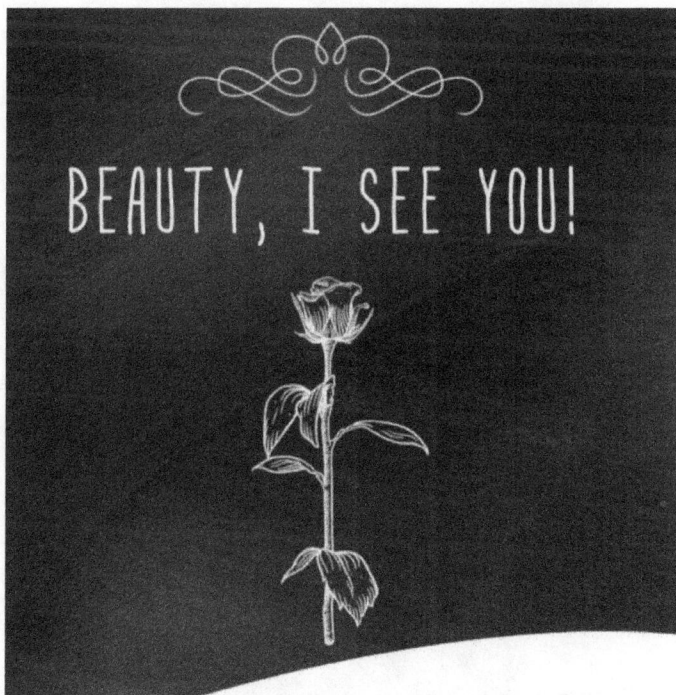

Pandora's Thought

We are holding back

So much adventure and beauty,

but who will wrestle us out of the arms of Pandora?

Part IV: Lost in Love

Through the Cracks

She could not see that she was broken beautifully
cracks in just the right places
Where the light could reach her

I Want to Love You

I want to love you back to me
the way the moon loves the waves back into the sea
With ease
They woo each other
endlessly into ecstasy
I want to
paint a pristine picture
of
you
That's seen
every time
they
look
at
me

One

I feel your pain brother
I am seeing that your blood is red,
That your struggles are mine and our successes are shared

****
****

-So often the world around us seems like it's in utter chaos.

During the occasions that we see people working together in love,
or witness someone esteem someone else higher than their own
selves, it is a beautiful thing.

Why are our timelines and everyday lives not flooded with these
types of experiences?

Egos, pride, and selfishness sometimes trump everything else in our
lives and in the lives of people we know.

We must be intentional about showing love.

We must be intentional in the acts of kindness that we show.
If we don't, then everyday concerns will drown the opportunities
we do have. Remember, it is evil not to empathize. We must love
and show grace constantly.

"The ground is most beautiful, when it is common"

Measure of Love

The sweetness
of God
Is measured
In kisses
And hugs
And warm
embraces and
liquid love

You

I am trying to get your attention.
I call but you don't hear me..only with your ears.
I am here but you are not looking..in the right places.
I'm running after you, but you are running, too...from the things
that I have planned for you.
Only look and you would see me. Think! And you would perceive
me. Turn, and I would heal you.
I am looking for you ALL the time.
I think of you and it makes me smile. Your joy radiates my heart.
You are in my consciousness endlessly, you never slip away from
my intimate desire.
The question I have for you is, What do you want from me?
You, is what I want from you.
Your passionate praise going out before the nations, your solemn
worship that you offer in surrender.
Your laughter as it pours over your heart like liquid love.
Your banner of righteousness that you fearlessly wave before men.
If I was hungry I would not tell you. If I was tired you would not
know it.
I tell you now that I am sovereign, but all I need is you.
A dying prince hung on a tree but cared enough to rise again.
A delicate rose fell to the ground, but was rustled up by the spirit of
love.

• • •

I am not satisfied without you, for I am always in pursuit of you.
I'm moving mountains, breaking bars of iron, and tearing down
walls just to be near you.
I'm in hot pursuit and I almost have you..right in the position that
you need to be.
Though I sit on a throne amidst a multitude of angels, though I am
warmed by the robes of decadent kings and queens; I am captivated
when I hear you;
Your words, captured in the sands of time.
I get excited when you praise..jubilant when you worship.
When I am moved with awe, I join you, to have the pleasure of
experiencing true love.
I am married to my mission,
and impassioned with my pursuit,
that one day out of your own heart,
and out of your own lips,
you would look up to the Heavens and say,

"All I need is you, Lord."
"All I need is you."

The Fire

People look toward its wonderment
drawn in by its warm embrace
As people are captured in the lure of its beauty,
so it is with God toward us.

The Greatest

The greatest love there ever was

dripped out upon a wooden cross

It was trapped between the cross-hairs

of ignorance and hate

but loudly proclaimed His mercy and grace

God Laughs

When God smiles.

His grin goes ear to ear.

A hearty rumble forms deep in his belly.

A harmonious melody is belted out,

And then it rains.

To Love

To love

Step out there

And offer your full self.

Love offered true will return to you.

Receive it daily as a gift, use it greatly to uplift

all those who cross your path.

Love does not hold a grudge, and

Love does not judge.

Love truly loves

Love until it hurts.

Love until it births something bigger than yourself.

Love completely without requiring reciprocity .

Accept the sorrows as learning experiences,

Know that love does disappoint but you are not expecting
perfection.

Let love erase the sorrows and fill them with joy.

Let love bring clean slates into tomorrows

Then replace the hopelessness with selflessness.

Oh, come with me and embark on the journey of a life time

What a great journey it is…

To love.

Sheltered

We stay sheltered in grace
And shame cannot
contaminate

Running

I'm running to the ends of the earth
That I may find you
Where men have failed to find you before

Love Is

Love is **eyes** that **see**

Arms that **reach**

Hearts that **speak**

And **Lungs** that **breathe**

…**deeply**

Scarlet:

Jesus wrapped

scarlet

around the hearts

of

harlots

-He wasn't afraid to approach the ones who society deemed unapproachable. He was always approaching them showing love through words and actions. He took their hearts and He was careful with them. Where they were wounded, He stitched them up.

The Chase

As I draw near

He draws close

Never do I appear as close as Id like

The closer I get—the further away I realize I am

I run toward Him, and cannot catch Him

He lets me catch Him

And I still want to be closer

Mosaics

God is still making mosaics
Out of broken glass

-Just because you're broken doesn't mean that God isn't using you to make a major impact. Even though the mosaic is made of broken pieces, the light gets through, and God loves that.-

The beauty that we're lost in is not held
hostage by hate, or brokenness or pain
It is a beauty forced into flame by
love.

Thank you for reading my first book of poetry!

I have been passionate about writing for a long time and am excited about being able to share this project with you!

I hope that these words were encouraging, thought-provoking and meaningful to you.

I am currently working on several other projects for the future, so stay tuned.

Also, I would love to get any feedback or questions that you may have.

Send me a message and reach me at the channels below.

Thanks again!

Lastly, if you have appreciated this work, please share!

Dorian Culver

Email: deculver25@hotmail.com

Instagram: @dec.33 or instagram.com/dec.33

Acknowledgments:

I want to thank everyone who has encouraged and supported me along the way.

I want to thank God, the originator of all gifts.

Thank you for allowing me the ability to create.

About the Author:

Dorian Culver

Dorian is a writer who is passionate about using his words to encourage others. He desires to help others develop their gift of writing and find platforms to share their work. He is the product of a military family and spent the majority of his childhood living in Germany. He is currently working on several writing projects to be released in the near future.

www.ingramcontent.com/pod-product-compliance
Lightning Source LLC
Chambersburg PA
CBHW071904020426
42331CB00010B/2663